Crying Flower Petals

Crying Flower Petals

Selected Poems, Essays and Memories

Scott Isaly

Copyright © 2016 by Scott Isaly.

Library of Congress Control Number:		2016906770
ISBN:	Hardcover	978-1-5144-8805-8
	Softcover	978-1-5144-8804-1
	eBook	978-1-5144-8803-4

All rights reserved. No part of this book may be reproduced or transmitted in any form or by any means, electronic or mechanical, including photocopying, recording, or by any information storage and retrieval system, without permission in writing from the copyright owner.

Any people depicted in stock imagery provided by Thinkstock are models, and such images are being used for illustrative purposes only. Certain stock imagery © Thinkstock.

Print information available on the last page.

Rev. date: 06/10/2016

To order additional copies of this book, contact:
Xlibris
1-888-795-4274
www.Xlibris.com
Orders@Xlibris.com

CONTENTS

Prologue xi

Spirit Vase... 1
Shoenchen 2
Salmon Croquets 3
Unbound 4
Pastoral Transfusion 5
Sing For Your Supper 6
The Forgotten... 8
Winds 9
Rapture of the Bees 10
Melancholy Riff..11
Trumpeters 13
Bucket List 14
Star Gazer 15
Masquerade.. 16
Aspiration 18
Letter to my Son 19
Rorschach Soap Bubbles... 20
Parody of Frost.. 21
Fowl and Cat 22
Adagio 23
Relative Freedoms 25
Rubbin' on the Moon.. 29
Sixty Beats Per Minute 30
This Time 31
Glimpse 33
Lumps 35
Trendsetting 36

Crying Flower Petals	37
Candy Apple	38
Indian Corn	39
Father Oil	41
Big House	42
Mementos of Now	44
Yip & Howl	45
Flashback	46
Nine Mile Bank	47
Soul Food	48
The Sentinel	49
Volunteers	50
To Be or Not to Be Anemone	52
East & West	53
Luminous Fool	54
One Percent	55
Shit I Won't Do for God	57
Connectivity	58
Floater	59
Sunset	60
The Butterfly Effect	61
Life's Instructions	62
Depression	65
Invisible Hands	66
Would You Fill My Creel?	67
Valuation	68
A Country of Music	69
California Harvest Moon	70
Tuna	72
Good Intentions	74
Big Time Player	75
Clue	76
Extension	77
Asymptomatic	78
Wide Angle View	79
In Between	80

Coda 82
Changels 83
Mind the Wind 84
Autumn of Life 85
Twenty-fourth Street USA 87
To Touch a Soul 88
American Ascension 90

About the Author 91

For Family and Friends

Prologue

As a prisoner constantly bombarded with others' poetry, the hope for this work is to provide enjoyment, enlightenment, and encouragement. Many readers want to write, and may this book provide you with the impetus which was offered to me – in a workshop group. My greatest hope for you is, inspiration. I wish you thoughtful reading.
Then, share your story.

Scott Isaly

Spirit Vase

I'm a broken skeleton
living at the bottom of a dry well
surrounded by sand, coins, and gem shards
Every now and then I play a duet with Kokopelli
and the notes like so many bats
spring from the well and fly skyward
into the indigo dusk
If the aim and the spirit music is true
the ancestors in the stars will weep
filling the mouth and the walls will seep
then the spirits will form a line
by the Palo Verde tree
and one by one dip the bucket and fill their vase
and the confluence will be scooped away
Once again my bones will bleach
until next time comes
filling the well with
my water
my blood
my poem

Shoenchen

Quixotic meets mnemonic at the psychic confluence
I/we struggle to produce a keepsake that will influence
Something from nothing as cheap as dirt
as nubile as a college cheerleader's skirt
Triumphant as great grandmother's scratch-made cherry pie
As hard fought as a rugby try
Gentle as a lamb
Immense like a dam
Full of meaning, we endeavor to craft those play on words
In fact communal like roaming herds
Maybe this time something enduring is born
Lord has seen the personas I've worn
Yet without the skills of the stars
nevertheless a story in these scars
Silent screaming to be remembered when I'm gone
If for only this one; I've won.

Salmon Croquets

At one point in the movie **St. Elmos Fire**, a recently liberated character played by Ally Sheedy says, "This is the best peanut butter and jelly sandwich I have ever eaten". She tells us this is so, as it is her first food she paid for and prepared in her own new apartment. I always think of her when I make salmon croquets.

I assembled salmon croquets as my first meal in my first solo place. Mom got me started with "I don't know, I mix the fish with smooshed crackers, throw in an egg and bake them".

I always kept the same basic recipe but got it in my head that liquid smoke was a key missing ingredient. Since then I've decided that was wrong and have tried many variations.

Sea salt and pepper seem the tried and true methods but just now I'm thinking toasted cumin seeds next time and maybe some cilantro. At any rate, when I drain the can of salmon I always wonder at the fish species and about the process of catching and canning the fish. My mind drifts to better days spent on the ocean.

Mixing in saltine crumbs with egg and the spice du jour is done in a glass bowl. Using a biscuit cutter, I portion out the patties and lay them on a parchment lined baking pan, then in the oven for a while, until light brown and the egg is well cooked. I have never messed up a batch and they come out better than tuna casserole and they are easier to prepare.

Call me neurotic, but in a profound way, to me, they represent the best free life can be.

Unbound

No brain or skein can bind
no number or letter will justice do
no compass or map can find
no adjective or hue
and the stone was rolled back
a simple promise of you

Pastoral Transfusion

One day I will sit down with brush and pencil
and depict the rainbow trout above my stone mantle.

At an antique desk with a Tiffany lamp
I'll read and make cards that require a stamp.

Yes correspondence will be key in my life
to rage against losing those in it to strife.

And breath the fresh Montana air as I write
maybe feel debonair and mellow my spite.

Simple meals and poems I'll prepare,
of complicated circumstances - had more than my share.

I'll read as necessary, recharge the mind,
and among the first I'll write my kind.

My goal - to purge cancerous confusion
and allow my soul a pastoral transfusion.

As for the trout, I prefer I'd caught it
so that I might leave a nameplate on it.

Sing For Your Supper

Fishing the cosmos
a bobber floats
on the river of souls
each with a life
and thoughts
that pull in the beginning

My mind's eye flies
between window bars
and searches for a life outside

Where the wild turkey
who sings a sweet song in distress
and clucks and gobbles
raucously when content

With the warning
of a prairie fire bearing down
causes us both to sing
But after eons of conditioning
For whom were the sweet songs meant?

For what in nature hears
a melody and thinks
"I need to render assistance."

Struggling with a metamorphosis
fishing line
the path is found

And the search for anomalies
continues in the soul currents
and into the chapel
Just as with the turkey
our songs play out our grievances
and torture

But, yet again
For whom were the sweet songs meant.

The Forgotten

Almost dawn again -
ephemeral, surreal, agitated gray
coming soon, revealing dust everywhere
and on the bottle.
Pounding headache, remnants of another magical manic night.
Expectations fading, the street sweeper
pushes aside the brothel erotica.
Her morning always starts on stained cigarette burned sheets.
Anticipating butts in the ashtray
moving to med line, she regards
a menthol in the corner outside her cell.
The match burns.
First smoke fills her head as bare feet
shuffle half naked to the street.
Scraping the grime out from under her fingernails - Someone
grabs her arm to usher her through the meal line.
Eyes water, as an angel sits down to eat in
the company of the forgotten.

Winds

Winds oft' blow in strange
ways.
I suppose that's why I choose
to face them every day.
The awkward first,
painful last,
and the eddies.
Thoughts more like the wind
than a carnal dance.
I knew nothing
yet knowing not
for only a time.
Else bending like the
Evergreen.
And the wind, thoughts, and her
immutable
things to behold.

Rapture of the Bees

All right, who fucked up?
I mean, was it a new formulation for pesticide?
Or perhaps a change to the harvest to render the seeds unusable.
Maybe the airwaves are too full to communicate and navigate.
Is it too hot?
Was money an issue?
It seems that healthy larvae lay abandoned in their cells.
Most of the worker bees, if not all, are dead, gone, or very ill - as with insect aids, in some places.
A bee died in front of me stinging a building the other day.
Okay, meet me halfway; there is a monolithic problem, right?
Healthy, abandoned larvae lead me to believe that the problems - do not commute in the hive, and the bees, for some reason,
do not return home to die,
Some areas are reporting ninety percent losses in their colonies.
Let's see - social, hard working, peace loving, die if they inflict harm, nurturing, organic, builders, live in a structured dwelling, organized living, provide society with a vitally important service.
Yeah, I see it now.
God called them home.

Melancholy Riff

She played the blues horn,
coronet, and man, you could hear
the cries of the world
in one riff.

Scales they're tippin'
Bad loans
and the banks are failin'
rumblin' tumblin'

Showgirls are glitterin' and bouncin'
Porn proliferatin'
Half the college students - bisexual
and sex slaves are laborin'
rumblin' tumblin'

World's gettin' hotter,
Honeybees in a flower
canaries of the hour
rumblin' tumblin'

Twin towers came down
War in ancient lands
bodies in the river abound
suicide bombs in the sand
half the world hates us
rumblin' tumblin'

AIDS, starvation, disease,
dirty politics, and warlords
In ten years time half the natives, now refugees,
won't be there for us
rumblin' tumblin'

Dead immigrant's bodies
at the border.
Kids buried by the Rio Grande
From Guatemala and El Salvador
died in trucks and made it to
the promise land.
rumblin' tumblin Devil go 'way

We pray with our actions
rumblin' tumblin' stumblin' home.

Trumpeters

He said that I brought them down
to witness my solo in front of a couple
hundred people in town
Uncanny how good I felt for once in my life.
My lips melded with the horn and my whole
body was singing the notes without strife
For a moment things were sublime as was the applause
I felt one with a just cause
Chuck Mangione the god of melodious tone
and there was Maynard Ferguson who could
scream the high notes and compose
Miles Davis made magic seem effortless
Dizzy Gillespie whose jive and jazz were electrifying
and finally there was Wynton Marssalis –
a true master craftsman with all styles classic and jazz
I borrowed from them all
So when I testify at the pearly gates of St. Peter
I'll remember this tune and beg of him one crutch
'Cause my words and deeds didn't amount to much.

Bucket List

I desire to know how birds decide
who to henpeck
Is it as arbitrary as religion
or always the runt
I want to eat duck comfit in Paris
a bucket of fried chicken in bed
Dim Sum in Korea, Sushi in Japan
and a Big Mac in China
I want to resurrect Steve Perry and
go to a Journey concert
I really want a certain five seconds of
my life back to do over
I want to fly in space
I want to save the human race
I want to master a computer language
I want to fly fish in Montana for trout
and 100 miles offshore for tuna
I want to play five different golf courses
and take pictures of wild horses
I want to visit famous art galleries
and shop flea markets, second-hand stores, and
auctions for items about which I can write
fictional stories
when life ceases to henpeck me
I want to do and write about it all.

Star Gazer

The past comes hurtling towards you
Ancient light from the heavens finally making the trip
One grain of sand amongst all the beaches on earth
and we like to think we are special
Ever expanding frontiers filled with the strange
and the relatively ephemeral
A vacuum filled with gas and rock and the atoms
that we are made of so long ago
Quasars, pulsars, black holes and dark energy
Even through different dimensions
Find man attempting to explain our origins
Sorting through the nearly infinite possibilities
and particles of our existence in relation
but if not for His signature
then whose?

Masquerade

Like the ones we will wear later in life,
the first one we try on
is an important part to our costume.

With the princesses, pirates, Storm Troopers,
and Power Rangers, among the old favorites.

A magical night through young eyes
to be sure,
yet there is more.

Concealed by a mask,
ethnicities and demographics are
a less pervasive element.

Here on our doorstep are disparate characters,
assembled in hordes,
yelling for candy;
gathered together somewhat free of
prejudice, and part of a new splendid
whole.

Some of us later than others,
grow into our teenage fascination
with the mask. Remember KISS?
A time to experiment with hair and makeup.
To follow social and industrial flash.

Throughout the ages,
and around the globe,
for a myriad of reasons,
most have donned a different look
for ceremony, concealment, or simple conformity.

Imagine for a minute,
how many instances you have seen.
Even as masquerades in America.
Where, after a fashion, and all grown up, we will
meld into a glorious whole, and
Beg for candy wherever it may be found.

Aspiration

The heart wants what the heart wants.
As does the hunter swing in a wide arc the downed Inca dove
splattering ink blots on his canvas.
A chef coaxes the starch from a grain of rice.
As does the spy pour over ciphers
to construct a meaningful message.
The pop artist delivers a fusion of Jazz and Soul.
the photographer strives to leave a lasting impression.
A king, doctor, soldier, lawyer, mother, father, child.
Paramount, while we are here we can concern
ourselves with this world.
So it is, the inmate, in a dreary dreary circumstance and curse,
endeavors to write verse.

Letter to my Son

Into the world comes a beautiful bundle of wants and needs.
My baby shakes his fist in the air,
as if to say I'll get you yet.
Upon first sight he looks like a ninety year old man,
burning in flames.
Ominous, and ninety years is a long time.
What will I tell him about the universe?
The day you were born was bright with sunshine.
I prayed you would be healthy all of the previous night.
You see, I adored you to the stars and back
before I even met you.
When you arrived my whole life changed.
I was truly blessed with the most well-behaved baby I ever met.
Growing up so fast, you left me with nothing but
joyous memories.
Experiencing the zoo animals together in spite of hard times-
the backyard swing set building party-
Trips to the beach, river, and lake to feed the ducks
and our souls.
Perhaps most of all, meals around the dining room table,
or any table.
To name a few.
From diapers to a straight backed, slightly rebellious,
extremely smart, young man.
And for your life experiences-
a labor of love.
Sleep peacefully little man at the end of each day.
No matter what, you are cherished, and an ardent admirer is
on your side, for life.

Rorschach Soap Bubbles

To create another realm by meter
and set the mood by rhyme.
How now do we describe the Spirit
of light in the moon?
Like peeling back layers of spray paint,
little trod path of immortality,
a covenant left by the Bard
even as we rest our feet upon his grave.
Tiny bucky balls assembling,
while our daily endeavors find us imagining
a shared reality, soaring over Mount Everest
as massive snow drift ridges
rise from below
assembling them bubble by bubble
flake by unique magic flake
while icicles drip nearby.
As usual, I can not be consoled by
the tug of this missive
and I reach for another soiled pan.

Parody of Frost

What prize is this that I have won?
To abide the southern California sun.
Cold and snow doeth surely inspire,
in winter I find the need to perspire.
With heavy pen I wait for a blow.
or anything else likened to snow.
While local hiking uncovers cactus.
How the old forests have come to impact us.
A writer might wait for a wintery bliss,
Or wear shorts at night during one's first kiss.
The ladies jeered at me as if I'd sinned.
The right to desire weather they would quickly rescind.
What stars in a forest filled with Frost and danger.
Or live many years, your neighbor a stranger.
As does the poet write to understand.
Great writing without weather-too much to demand.
So day turns to night and on and on,
I wonder, is my soul, like the forests, partially gone.

Fowl and Cat

Come fill the old feeder in a paper birch tree.
On a still, white, winter morning, a scene to see,
and lie prone inside with my furry friend Ko.
What happens next he has come to know.
Soon, in a frenzy, would be cardinals, finches, wrens and bluebirds.
The sight itself defies words.
By the heater vent behind a glass door,
maneuvering for a vantage to see more.
Enthusiasm builds as he wiggles his haunches,
preliminary to his feline launches.
Some seed spills over to the snow
where chickadees feed down below.
Oblivious to all but the spectacle, he gets excited
the door, and he, are swiftly, thud! united.
With the seed gone and the cat concussed
we view the chickadee tracks - the exhibit discussed.
Step after step shaking off paw
we leave fresh tracks as he dreams of feathery maw.
Another day tomorrow, that
we can entertain fowl and cat.

Adagio

Delicately, Softly
rouse all the senses.
A trepidatious staccato
footfall
crunches into another world.

Slowly trees sway as if
in a melodic current
and with every gust
leaves rustle like
thousands of tiny castanets.
I come frequently to gaze at
the orchestration of a
forest without fences,
a phrase without end.
Brilliant September leaves,
fire amber, clay red, and earth brown,
settle, as if cued,
testament to Life's cycle.
The essence of nature's mulch
pervades the air.
There is dew in the frigid morning and
breath plumes are visible;
parsing our time together.

Steadfast Guardians of the woods
reach up from the
unction of the floor
to the tree tops and beyond
in a crescendo of a
clouded sky Exhibition!
Stars of the symphony -
cherry, walnut, oak, paper birch, maple, and apple,
transform with the seasons in unique
dramatic fashion.
Offer us sustenance.
While the evergreen, immutable,
provides stability to the Gathering.

Down below, roots conduct the Coda, the
basis of life, of being enveloped by
Nature's strain.

Relative Freedoms

Our father
there is fire burning,
an undertone to all that we are
soul churning

Who art in heaven
a dark musical melody
reminding us,
when we pious dare listen,
of relative freedoms

Hallowed be thy name
Evermore we need be reminded
time by time
of circumstances in life
not yours or mine

Thy kingdom come
of a Darfur refugee to
have a cell with a key,
TV, yard time, and three,
squares a day
no Janjuweed

Thy will be done
Guatemalan girl
working for minimum wage
the promised land for a temporal sage

On earth
a serf to cultivate
his own fiefdom dreams
centuries old,
or not it seems

As it is in heaven
away from the gangland machetes
of Brazil or Nigeria
perhaps to succumb to
cholera or diphtheria

Give us this day
A Lebanese farmer
longs to sell his produce abroad
no market he'll find for tilling
radical sod

Our daily bread
escape from political oppression and genocide
time without disease or illness
suicide

And forgive us our trespasses
away from those who prey on children
for sex or labor
often overlooked by a powerful neighbor

As we forgive those
widening disparity
between rich and poor
middle class jobs shipped overseas
out the door

Who trespass against us
Mountain Dew in
a sippy cup, diabetes
has descended upon
American families

Lead us not into temptation
world free of
terrorism, sectarian violence,
civil war,
and suicide bombs
often set in motion
with childlike aplomb

But deliver us from evil
the paralyzed long to move
instinctively
or even speak succinctly

For thine is the kingdom
Environmental rape
does now raise hairs on the nape

The power
narco-trafficers across the border
making a mockery of law and order

And the glory for ever and ever
a few blessings bestowed
on many of us
unless we choose to forget
hardships avoided
never mind jurisprudence,
and pray for relative freedoms
anointed

Amen

Rubbin' on the Moon

We're rubbin' on the moon
There's a hurricane blowin' bassoon
we real big, we bad
Now cavorting with the stars
Tear drops and tsunami's upon thars
we real big, we bad
Tiptoeing through amber grain fields
Sustained on the bounty a toy train yields
we real big, we bad
Dodging satellites
Deadly diversions for socialites
we real big, we bad
We now need a community in space
Aspirations without charity, a disgrace
we real big
Look, a young woman, my creator, pull me down
Pull me down by the numbers
Cause, ask Icarus, too high we fly,
We're rubbin' on the moon

Sixty Beats Per Minute

As I fall forward into my meager life;
I've lost love.
And the space in my soul has occupied
the vacated area with "time tested loyalty".

There are, from time to time, memories
of you introducing me to my life; while
my heart has become a simple metronome,
a dead reckoning instrument,
keeping my time with a soul and marking
our existence together.

My chest no longer flutters and fancies
like in the college years.
As an ardent admirer, looking back
on the carnal dance not shared,
labels not applied,
things have not been right.
tick
tick
ticking
since counting perfect time,
with loyal you.

This Time

Most often I sit down to write feeling like a monkey scribbling ink out of spite.

I mean, is it possible for an addled, sleep-deprived, mediocre mind to produce a great poem by outworking the greats?

I can't imagine the process is much different for he and she as it is for me.

Somewhere in the bowels of the spirit a kernel of inspiration is grasped, then amplified by the heart, and refined by the mind, and just like that, out it comes, right? on to the paper.

What was the creative process behind a rouge more perfect and temperate than a rose.

Or a fog likened to cat feet.

An elusive fox of an idea.

These feelings I have, or to some degree agree with, but my written word is lost in the ether.

While the soul of great poets finds the practical words to describe interesting thinking.

Do I have access to the same inspiration?

Hell yes, I have been in love, but I run low on original similes and metaphors.

You see I not only want to be good, but great.

I tend to want to create some otherworldly description so as not to be blasé.

I am trying to learn to use plain old words with multiple meanings.

Man, I mean, they don't have to even be whole words or even make sense to convey my soul's language.

To avoid the sad fact that I will never be one of the greats, I am tempted to create my own language.

Rah cryin' flower petals sae
two is he as Rumbah she
ola we go
we go
no mo

Dammit, God just give me one.

This time.

Glimpse

An occasion to open the door to my mind
When keeping it closed seems more kind

A lack of imagination I've never had
But a peek inside could turn out bad

The question is begged - what to share
or should I let all fly on a dare

A glimpse of what went in to making a psyche
A long strong education is the beginning of my key

It is true I graduated from the University
But my curriculum was a study in unfocussed diversity

A lack of focus seems a common theme
In fact, it's a good bet for my requiem

A puny Progress I've made is due to tenacity
it seems much more valued than my mind's capacity

Enough with the past and puttering about
It's time to let a few tidbits leak out

I have been called every name in the book
Yes, even the worst, and so far none have took

As far as I can tell
this is the way minds bend to hell

You see I have lost nearly everything I've cared about
To make sure, it seems, I gathered no clout

I loved not wisely and perhaps too much
Lord knows I've lost the midas touch

So here I stand convicted of a crime
The product of nothing good coming with time

Recently I've come to grips with my mental state
Whether the illness will pass, I can only wait

Not a day goes by I am not filled with fear and regret
A tormented mind just not dead yet

Imagine if you will, a suicidal lilt
Playing always in the background regardless of what I built

A few seconds of madness on this I'm defined
now twenty-seven years I will be confined

Imagine the gloom which overshadows every task
If you'd like to know, brave soul, about specifics, just ask.

Lumps

Boiling milk in a better time
Add cream of wheat
while attempting to ignore all of the dirty dishes in the sink
Barely stir to produce the desired nickel circumference lumps
The trash is overflowing again
If the lumps are too big they are dry in the middle - too small
and they aren't really lumps
The linoleum floor tiles are coming up
I miss the decorative plates hung high on the walls – some semblance of order
And you, I miss you
Add butter pat and brown sugar upon plating
I still eat cream of wheat once a week
but needless to say, dear boy, no one makes the lumps for me.

Trendsetting

You can't beat his trending
but some fault his spending.
With health care he'll trim the fat
While aging Boomers
believe that's not where the fat's at.
So three cheers for Obama
a health bill he'll pass
and trend where others
fell flat on their ass.
Now if only the economy would revive
attending Dr. Obama
will bring it alive.
So three cheers for Obama
The wars he'll see end
Our steadfast aplomb
soon he will bend.
So three cheers for Obama
The confident of schools
support will be given
within the rules.
Three cheers for Obama
Torture is in the past
for our great nation state
We may indeed last.
One, two, and three cheers for Obama
Who represents well with his graceful mate
his capacity for hope
may release us from yesterday's
blind fate.

Crying Flower Petals

In meeting you, my senses were born again.
I never saw the sun till I watched it set with you.
Scintillating new horizons with pink-red and golden hue.
Yes, I never felt the ocean till I swam in it with you.
Waves crashing on the sand beneath a sky of deep blue.
And I never heard the music till I danced to it with you.
Side by side we played duets till our dreams all came true.
Details of affirmation abound like a wink from a dove.
Infinite muse, love with you, is a blessing from above.

Candy Apple

One more step -
irregular -
sliding towards a candy apple.
Circus atmosphere -
Carnies hawking their wares to the buzz
against blaring rock music
and walls of stuffed animals.
Lights strung around the arcade.
greasy food, cotton candy, popcorn and electric air-
rides streaked with multi-colored bulbs.
The Octopus - a spindly semaphore
The Sled - for four tickets
Ferris wheel - to new views
Food, arcade, and animal stench
Musty arts and crafts shows
Abandoned racecourse out back
A respite for making out in the stands
Hole in the fence
One last step to reality
Next time, Poet, come with me and try a candy apple,
or something else special found
without deliberate venture.

Indian Corn

Morning ride,
full of brutal anticipation.
three miles from canoes on the Mohican River.
Ethereal mist envelops a corn field, nestled in woods,
as if at any moment an ancient chief's
spirit would appear.

Balmy day, parsed only by the songs of neighboring birds in witness trees.
Fueling an air of Native American mysticism.
The scene makes us feel we will unearth
a sacred find.

Freshly turned earth
plowed under corn stalks
broken like skeletons and half buried
amongst raised relics of
inhabitants past.

Dewdrops once found on unfurling corn silk
of baby sweet white corn
drawing up sustenance from the stewards of long ago.

Gingerly, row by row,
combing the soil for worked flint or stone,
even a spirit vase
lodged in the damp musky soil.
Imagination conjures
communal grinding stones, hunts, and lives past.

Despite the excitement of new finds
our spirit sags at the realization of uprooted peoples.
Bound to history, we find
arrowheads, grinding stones, a shark's tooth.
Left to wonder what shock and awe campaign was waged
on these early natives.

Father Oil

Primordial ooze
Foundation of Industry
arterial flow of progress
mover of people
fuel of all work

Demand and supply coming to a pricey head
time to find a new way
Dark brown as the eyes of a veiled desert princess

Bombs on the pipeline
Great hammers seem to bow
like an answer to a prayer call
Enabler of kingdoms
molder of governments
smog maker to the world

Primordial ooze
Foundation of Industry
arterial flow of progress
mover of people
fuel of all work
Mother Earth, Father Oil

Big House

Stuffed full of self-loathing and consumed by remorse
it can be excruciatingly lonely

                                                                     in this

house full of souls

Long halls stacked with reeking cells
could be a row of tiny townhouses

                                                                     but

for dreams deferred

placed mostly against will by the weakest Judge
and a system of degenerate competition
we often find ourselves seeking anodyne escape
some more than others compound their sins
esoteric condemned pour their heart out with pen or brush
and late at night while there is a hush
We want for sleep and the lord or soul to keep
while mothers wait out the cruel moments
and fathers try not to weep for children

  left

simply, when we are acclimated, of hope one is bereft.

So let it be known to those who dare

                                                    Pass
by the big house

count your blessings and say a prayer

                                                    for

the reticent.

Mementos of Now

Wisps of you flickering in my mind.
Curiosities of minutiae resounding
brilliantly. Painfully.
Like it was only minutes ago we were together.
A love before true cruelty is known.
Older now, driven insane by the loneliness.
Dementia takes me farther away from you.
Not many dated, but a million eyes seen,
never a one as keen.
The silver has lost its' luster.
Tiny cracks in the porcelain face.
Meals never taste quite right without footsies under the table.
Old music, our music, is given a new life.
Still waiting for a one ring signal.
Slow dancing, essence of you, nestled in your neck.
Mementos of now.
Like so many pressed wild flowers
in my favorite book of life.

Yip & Howl

I could actually see the starlight dance in her eyes
On a moonlit night in the Tucson foothills
The desert was alive with magic and the
yip and howl of the coyotes captured my attention.
A primal outpouring of religious fervor,
likely aimed at the moon.
We might find the same dynamic in
a choir of a Southern Baptist Church
Or in a group of drunken frat boys
ogling a pretty woman to make the sounds
one might expect the vocalizations of a tribe
celebrating a hunt to howl thusly
or from a ululating widow.
Moreover we have developed inhibitions
that prevent us from singing out on a regular basis.
The coyotes let it rip regularly and nightly
and with the twinkle of a diamond pendant
around her neck my fugue is broken
amongst mesquite trees, rock formations, and saguaro cactus.
I find myself better off for being with her
and even let out a little yelp of my own.

Flashback

Looking back I see a young blond one
holding a sparkler in DC.
It was the Fourth, by Freedom Lake at dusk.
and the opulence of memorials abounds
the pomp and circumstance of the capitol resounds.
Black and white memories of family and
spaces with cherry trees are what I have left
If I could go back, would I tell the little
boy the truth?
About how life can be cruel and melancholy.
Would I interrupt the fireworks shine upon shine
And explain the illness that is all mine.
I once was happy and wouldn't change a thing
Should I tell him life is precious like a ring.
Now listen to me, just before it burns out,
give the sparkler a fling.

Nine Mile Bank

When it's hot the bold and beautiful
strut their stuff down a watery arcade.
Marlin, like kings, wield their swords
through schools of bonito and mackerel
feasting on the wounded.
Various species of tuna chase
great balls of anchovy and sardines
that twinkle in the mayhem like silver and gold coins.
The seagulls and sharks - one from above
and one below clean up the carnage.
While the sunfish, a grotesque, hangs
around like a bearded lady
the flying fish take great leaps
skimming over the swells.
The dolphin frolic like courtier jesters
When it's cold, you can find a grey whale,
the great Leviathan, arching and fluking
in all of its dragon-like splendor
and at the end of the day, the stately
sea lions lounge on a buoy, taking it all in.

Soul Food

Only sometimes I think
I have a soul

mostly when it hurts

and turmoil has wrest it
from my person

my head and heart never
in sync

But one usually wins out
a shallow victory at least

Souls don't need food
and I need to have butternut squash again

So much left to experience
like the squash, brown sugar, butter, currants

Makes it almost okay
to save my provisional soul for a better day.

The Sentinel

Equally at ease in Heaven and hell and
wired like an alien
Always obeys the law of the land
He sees a threat in a baby's bassinet
and will act friendly to a lunatic
Always the first to know what the breeze brings
Perfectly willing to step into the line of fire
Stand his station all day and never tire
Seen by society as a needed part
but loved by no one deep in the heart
He is sure to have human needs
but if anyone sees them fufilled, he bleeds
Ever important in the perilous future
Guarding the rich, guarding our children.

Volunteers

My name is Johnny Blue Shirt and I will be the first capital punishment volunteer; with the following stipulations.

The DA's and bureaucrats that pass multi-decades indeterminate sentences and unconscionable 15 year denials need to make sure they get it right. Trials go by without fairness every day. If balance and justice be done, there need be a period of positive affirmation to demonstrate the good life one might have led - in contrast to a very brief few seconds in which a crime was committed. Did one ever save lives, or raise a family, hold a job, be a mentor, a sibling? I mean, I picture the grandeur of an American idol type televised feature of prospective volunteers. In this more public forum, and you know people would tune in, a montage of the incarcerated man's life other than the crime would be celebrated publicly. Without false allegations and vitriol, perhaps culminating in a few words direct to the viewing audience or reading an appropriate poem - creating a humane environment.

The show would, in a life-affirming manner, introduce to the public a real view and could go on tour searching out the best stories. Paramount, every volunteer would be afforded a very public forum.

Furthermore, a sum of one hundred thousand dollars should be paid to my family or say ten percent of what keeping me incarcerated would cost; In compensation for saving the state a million or so for a life sentence.

When a cooling off period and a public show of who someone really is has been achieved; I want to check out the same way I went out with general anaesthesia - counting backward from ten and suddenly I am no longer.

If this sounds far-fetched - look at the suicide statistics in prison. Take a look at the cruel and unusual sentences getting passed. The private sector would bear the cost of the publicizing period. I feel that every time a life sentence or a significant time is handed down, more time should go into what life is.

Personally, I would play a blues song, read some Frost to the world along with something I wrote then check out on my own terms.

So in the spirit of the **Hunger Games** one is allowed to have real emotions about the volunteers.

My name is Johnny Blue Shirt and I will be the first capital punishment volunteer.

To Be or Not to Be Anemone

Beneath my shimmering reflection
tiny concentric neon blue arms
undulate as if conducting
a symphony in the miniature coliseum
of a tide pool teeming with life.
As the water ebbs
the exposure causes a complete retraction
until the tide rolls back in
bringing new life, new promises
and finds the arms reaching for sustenance
waving about on gentle currents.
Some visitors find shelter within
others - poisonous barbs for the cycle of life
If by the Gods it were meant to be
I would come back as one
so similar it and me.

East & West

I remember a huge tongue of bronze
spilling from the crucible.
A Buddha five stories tall becoming the
sheer immensity of a jovial God
leaves you smiling.
I remember the Shinto shrines
represented by many Gods and ancestors
some temples you place burning joss sticks
and watch the smoke carry your prayers heavenward.
Idols that require a monetary gift
to facilitate your dream wishes
or commit prayers to paper and post.
All human friendly interpretations of the Almighty.
By contrast, many of us grow up
bearing a torture device
or being offered the symbolic Body and Blood
of the Son of God
leaving no way to live but sin
and ask for forgiveness.
I can't help but be hopeful for the eastern incarnations
put off by a heavenly entity telling me Eat me.
I remember asking for a translation of a
menu in Seoul - we found the item we
had hoped for to be a fried slug
To each his own.
I guess one could do worse than bread & wine.

Luminous Fool

Pray like today is your last day.
Live like it isn't.
They will show you how.
Time after time the tenth step is
lost.
Even as they pluck a first completion.
Like playing a game of chess against
a mind reader.
It's all a show.
Made up of the quixotic adventures
by the Luminous Fool.
And in our Folly we delve into the
vein-like complexity of the current
matter at hand.
Fleetingly organic.
Until the caw, caw, caw of Poe's
raven is like the ethereal
enumeration of our soul-fest
And at the end of the day
nature watches us pray
like today is our last.

One Percent

Disclaimer: Facts and figures may be
distorted as often happens these days.

Far less than one percent represents the
people who will attend an OWS protest.

One percent represents our all volunteer
military who despite its directives we can
all agree is full of heroic people.

Less than one percent represent the citizens
who are willing to be arrested and clash
with peacekeepers.

Medical doctors make up less than one
percent of the population and depending on
speciality and work ethic, may also qualify
for their well deserved one percent.

One percent may decide to become college
professors and be very important as gate keepers.

Funny how far less than one percent
claim to speak for the ninety-nine percent. Isn't that
a remaining problem here?

One percent represents the incarcerated population,
and trust me, it's not all it's cracked up to be.

Less than one percent are politicians
who deserve a lot of the blame these
days at least as far as fiscal responsibility is
concerned, but nonetheless, they are willing to serve
The public and they did form a more perfect union.

One percent represents the police force on overtime to
keep the peace at "peaceful" protests and spraying the
grandmas with pepper spray.

the whole world knows - one, regardless of caste position,
can always strive to be in the top one percent in school, work,
and other endeavors in this - our great country.

So you see, one can always aspire to the one percent in some form.
However, if your Robin Hood ethic finds you
obsessing about money, ask yourself as you bang the drum,
are you in the one percent?

Shit I Won't Do for God

25 years, the subject of a Fengsha
a ban on a person and his work.
The term literally means, "seal off to kill".
Left with time to contemplate the entities that have dominion over you
and wonder if there is any way to get back into good graces.
So you, in effect, try and work backdoor deals with him or her
As if it matters, I mean, inevitably you learn about what you
are or are not willing to go along with for pantheism.
Is anything about me going to propitiate them?
So my divination is this.
I won't manufacture bombs physically or spiritually; bombs are an affront to the innocent.
Jihad by any other name I won't inflame.
Ruining someone verbally or otherwise to suicide, I won't abide.
Managing populations without edict spurs conflict.
Mob thinking in important times will lead to crimes.
I will not live another's life.
He will never again reduce me to an animal.
Shades of grey are merely shadows for the devil to hide in.
Society may ask, "We're left with who?"
Wise as a serpent, gentle as a dove.
For God, when push comes to shove, there is shit I won't do.

Connectivity

In a land where no food grows
the shifting sands whirl and shape
life anew each day.
Tiny grains like
so many bits and bytes in our modern psyche
we see now that a bronze spear
is emerging for the people.
Not a weapon in and of itself
though it likely was meant to be.

Floater

Well, so it is, I'm 42
I beg of him, there are
things I want to do
a pilgrimage, perhaps,
to the holy land
photograph the ground of Jesus' last stand
maybe pen a tweet so profound
Peace will break out the whole world round
meet a man on his way to Hades
whose blood is miraculously immune to AIDS
Sip a black and tan, and talk
to an ice-cream head woman with a leggy walk
Fish marlin in tropical seas
or tie a fly, a rainbow trout tease
catch a symphony in a modern place
leave with a tune and my heart full of grace
happen upon love's wild mustangs by a stream
A fleeting moment - much as life's Requiem
When my head's all full of razors and nooses
ankles, wrists, and throat.
I offer a pensive l'chaim
and make excuses, to stay
afloat.

Sunset

We can see the same sunset
snowy undulating clouds
like lemon lime cotton candy
tinged with pink and orange fire

Not unlike the quality and
scent of her hair
appreciated in a slow dance
a youthful embrace, so base

Words, over pizza and
soda with an ice cream mind
while the world was still kind
Soothing, even now, to remember

Then one day a dark welling inside
and it made her cry
a part of me the devil attends
secretly, quietly, we remain close friends

By me done of temporary pain
my crowning achievement, losing her,
and with one ring watched her fly
All the more beautiful to multiply

I weep for her every time
a muse or letter brings her around
like sacred music enveloping hers and more
and pray that we see a sunset
someday from the ground.

The Butterfly Effect

Strip miner of the crust
Smasher of the atom
Polluter of the earth

The spawning salmon swim up river
A hard hat fires up his mining apparatus
each year the water breathes more acrid
of storms and floods like God's global semaphores
a tiny eddy made by weary fin
like a butterfly stirring the air
and the complex attempt to overcome the small with big
life giving waters measure the will of man against
salmon to carry on

Strip miner of the crust
Smasher of the atom
Polluter of the earth

Its smokestack against insects
and the fish's secret is that with or without
his barometer
Nature always has the last laugh

Life's Instructions

I was eight.

Ordinarily, a shopping trip for frozen chicken livers is not stimulating, unless it means a fishing trip to Navy Lake, with your dad, the next day.

After scarcely sleeping due to excitement, and rising early to get ready, it was time to load the bicycles with gear and supplies such as were found in a tackle box my great grandfather left us. Following close behind on my bicycle, I could take in the scenery and think about a fishing legacy. As we passed by a motocross track, or two horses mating in a pasture, I remember the oldest of lures tucked away in the old tin box. A fork in the road took us to the main lake to fish catfish; the other back lake was for bluegill.

On the main lake there were mist stalagmites seemingly propping up a fog cloud which enveloped us on a still, cool, morning. As if on a stage, fog left us on our own closed set, blotting out the rest of the world. Circular ripples are the only sign of life in the water as distant waterfowl parse the morning with their calls. There is a small tide moving against the shore as a water moccasin slithers in. From our vantage point, small reed islands in the middle of the lake are barely perceptible through the haze.

Trial and error has made us very adept at catfishing and bonding a singular relationship. We have tried everything, including attempts at fish clubbing with a canoe paddle that was to no avail. We always sat on an old park bench that jutted out into the lake. To bait our treble hooks with frozen chicken livers meant carving off a frozen hunk and affixing it to the hook fashioned with a spring. A small split-shot clamp on weight about one and a half feet up the line from the hook, a Zebco push-button reel, and light line are all the gear we needed. With a gentle but firm cast, one is either successful or commits the hilarious mistake of having the bait fly farther than the hook. Well, it is hilarious unless you are the one who has to reel in and re-bait. Not much gear is required to fish for catfish but the tackle box we used contained lures of every shape and size, as well as flies for bass and trout. A small twisted piece of metal called a Z-ray, which is in the spoon family, is painted orange-red florescent and brings forth memories of Brown Trout in the White Mountains. Flies with colored feathers that match the hatch on different streams conjure up images of arching overhead casts to a specific pinpoint utilizing a fly rod and reel. Solid lures that are made to simulate fish, crawfish, even frogs, are primarily used to catch bass and pike in freshwater lakes. The best lures come in a variety of sizes and colors to catch fish in a multitude of water conditions; a chartreuse lure for murky water or a natural shad finish fo clear water. There are also jelly baits which simulate natural prey and have a consistency of strong Jell-o. With hooks properly joined to such lures, each can be deadly in a given situation. Lures are purchased in anticipation of having the right bait for a given body of water and sought after species of fish and usually are chosen based on word of mouth by local fishermen. There are many thousands of such lures available so one should have some idea of what they are looking for before shopping. Also, there are baits meant to go with a hook and sponge and formulated to match what these fish crave. For instance a bait called Mr. Stinky, a blood bait, is a favorite of catfish but frozen chicken livers are cheaper. Each lure, fly, or bait tell a story about future excursions.

There is an art to setting a hook when you get a nibble. In other words, the small catfish would nibble around the bait before taking the hook into its mouth. Consequently, one would allow the fish to pull out line or wait for the line to slacken, for three to five seconds before setting the hook and yelling, "Yeeeeeeehah...I got one!" Then the fight is on, which is fun when using light tackle and loose drags. When you get one to the shore, watch out for the spines in the fins; we handle the fish carefully with a towel and attach them to a stringer.

After a good morning of fishing, we ride back, catch in tow. when we get home we would clean the fish and I would suffer some psychic stress - cleaning and gutting fish while my dad once gave the sex talk: "When a man an a woman are in love..." While we were in the process of deciding where exactly to cut and sever the head, I find out that I may one day fall in love and have this thing called sex. Scooping out the entrails of a catfish and pondering how boys and girls are different seemed strange, even at the time where nothing is strange. At any rate, we both decided we had better concentrate on the mechanics of skinning the fish. The talk was quick, but not forgotten. Damn Horses! Nevertheless, usually we would just talk about school, the day, sports...a fishing legacy.
Life.

Depression

Something declared open season on my heart
I feel things are over without even a start
Like a sky burial in all of its grotesque wonder
A feeling that at 43 life was just a blunder
So cut me to pieces, see if I care
It beats the fresh new hell of which I've been made aware
Without love or people in my life
Severed with a big proverbial knife

Watching them fall ill
Looking for solace in a little white pill
From then to now there is no joy
Just a series of rules were taught to employ
So round up the vultures, eagles, and Raven
On second thought, perhaps, I'll just burn in my little safe haven

Invisible Hands

Father
What to do
With invisible hands?
Did they not hold
Your son at birth?
Did they not toil in
the fields?
Did they not play catch
in the great halls?
Did they ever think to
touch her cheek the
woman you knew and
loved but just missed
by an eternity?
What to do with Invisible
hands?
Did they ever touch
anything more tangible
than a soul.

Would You Fill My Creel?

Just about sunrise, merrily walking a rough footpath from cabin to stream.
From out of the fog a magnificent sight appears as if from a dream.
I spy a rainbow trout gliding against the current.
Should I present egg, nymph, or fly?
Effortlessly taking what may come tumbling to it.
Brilliant green speckled back, shimmering, holding against the tide.
Would you fill my creel?
Perhaps a spinner, spoon, or jig, should be cast nearby.
Until my rod tip is bent.
Maybe worm, corn, or cheese drifted down to him
as if heaven sent.
Even marshmallow, feed bait, or dough could be worth a try.
I think, instead, I will push aside my tackle, lean my rod against the bough, sit next to the jewelweed, and gaze in wonder at this neon blessing on which we rely.

Valuation

Speck of carrot
Small insignificant
Waste
Tiny little piece of
discarded trash, spit out
by a genetic engineer
as she ate the last subject
of a failed experiment
that -
tasted better when cooked
sweeter when fresh
full of antioxidants
grew bigger than others
grew faster
provided 100% RDA of vitamins
could eat the tops
make top juice packed full of vitamins
had a long shelf life
grew in the desert with no fertilizer and low water
helped with weight loss
cured AIDS and other illnesses
vaccinated against all major illnesses
slowed the aging process
Small, insignificant
little speck
last of your kind
worth more than my life.

A Country of Music

In this vast expanse of a country
From the diminutive cell of prison,
You can almost feel the strings
vibrating on a cellular level.
Music can be heard
changing from place to place.
Across the country the big cities - L.A., New York
set in a raucous cacophony of electric element.
The great plains ebb and flow
brightly like Vivaldi.
The South has a blues soul all its own - so many.
As all of the Northern states
change seasons with the finality of a Mozart piece.
The West in general is
well suited to the country music emanating forth.
And the industrious East shore
plays a steady thrum, thrum, thrum of industrial sound
though the trials and tribulations abound.
If you're careful
you too can hear the music from your area
like the Angels do on the Far Flung Shores at sundown
May God once again bless our country
and let the muse himself live amongst us.

California Harvest Moon

La Luna tiene una Corona cual se va por el empano de mi exhalacion in el vidrio de mi auto.
On the road from our temporary house to the mall parking lot, the world is bathed in the light of the harvest Moon, ephemeral, surreal in the early morning hours.
A short wait, then we board the old white bus with a green cross above the windshield at 4:30 am.
Now we are under way, in silence, to one of over seventy-five thousand farms in California.
Soon perfect rows delimit the landscape, and wind-blown crops bow and ripple in waves.
Eyes bright and sleepy, it is still grey out as we pull up to the field.
In the past we have worked: melons, tomatoes, tomatillos, broccoli, cauliflower, grapes, cucumber, oranges, lemons, grapefruit, avocado, nuts, peppers, leafy greens, and strawberries to name a few.
Today crews work side by side cutting, pitching, or packing to collect the harvest.
Moving as swift as able down the rows, we send finished packed product to the tractor pulled trailers.
As the day wears on the heat is stifling.
The vegetation is baked in the sun and hot humid air rises to our stooped faces with the smell of greenery.
We get paid for production: consequently, we push ourselves.
At the end of the rows the packing trucks get loaded with effort in our repetitive motions.
Semi-documented with papers purchased in Mexico we work for about minimum wage.
We keep a lookout for sidewinders, bees, and Border Patrol.
My family is all dark skinned with squinting facial lines.

There are calluses on our hands and most of us are in good physical shape.
Igloo coolers and porta-potties are the only amenities in the fields.
At some point we have handled most of the selections in the market produce section.
On the way back to the mall parking lot, after a long day,
we can once again see the Harvest Moon.
Imagine, I just handed you a ripe piece of produce.
You don't know who I am; because in effect, I did and you don't.
Twelve million of us provide some of your most vital services every day and 98% of your population growth is from immigration.
With a new emphasis on local, organic, sustainable produce, social engineering, and farm to table restaurants, we may one day meet, and perhaps share some salsa.
Until then, I will follow the harvest and live in my California, glowing in the moonshine.

Tuna

moving with us
new scintillating rays of light
from the other atmosphere
above, through the dark
swish, swish, swish
migrating fast

After much living has passed

small of us shimmering, food!
we break formation and attack
feeding with ferocity
Neon flash of us, quivering
swimming, again searching
for a kelp paddy
and more food

After much living has passed

progress of existence
brown muck on the coral
Past, present, and future
concerns, acidic ocean
Time to meet at the spawning place

After much living has passed

ride the warm currents
under whatever shade is possible
not as many of us
getting harder to breath
grow, swim, and repeat
swish, swish, swish
sometimes the big come
to feed on we little.

Good Intentions

With the best of intentions, at least
to their mind, the hijackers killed
thousands
With the best intentions, at least
in our mind, we killed a million
Forty thousand have died in the
struggle to supply the stockbroker and
waitress lines in the back of the bar
Genocide is a common term for
the best of intentions with regard
to birth rights
Blood diamonds and oil flow the
world round to our borders
with the intentions born of
necessity for governance regimes
kill protesters
with good intentions albeit
selfish, bankers manufacture poison securities
Best intentions keep millions incarcerated
Likely with the best of intentions
our leaders provide us security at
least for the rich and strong
Best intentions pilot missile carrying
drones to far away lands and
children stumble on cluster bombs
The reality is mind numbing
Best intentions for opportunity keep
many flocking to us through
the hand of the devil
I'm not sure about the road to
hell but the road to democracy
is surely paved with good intentions.
and its the best thing going.

Big Time Player

Mind's on the trigger of a shotgun
a scattershot
driving back briefly the impetus of life
until a crashing wave of pain
tumbles us back to reality.
You turn my eyes wrong.
A singular notion springs forth
hundreds of tiny self-reflecting mirrors
a projection from the barrel
and the tragedy of turning the gun on oneself
for all to see.
You turn my eyes wrong.
So do we reload
or hold fast as the
sweet release of our last endeavor...
and we play it straight.
You turn my eyes wrong.

Clue

Animal eyes and compunction to
use our crease of time
assembling what we will be
probing the ethereal for
titbits of interesting thought
like plucking ripe cherries
from a tree and popping
them in your mouth
or worrying, recording, forming
sweet product
asking with every tome
Is it good enough for them.

Extension

If you
don't watch
him, he'll
eat shards
of glass
one vaudevillian
truth
and thunder
forecasting the
dopamine plunder
As we
senile and
just
kill ourselves
with a lonely
thrust of nourishment
turned gluttony
simpler it would be
spanning ours
and his affecting each other
and all that there is.

Asymptomatic

As a young man throwing a cast-net into the Gulf of Mexico with shrimp boats on the horizon against an orange sunset.

Or in the thin mountain air holding a girl, by the lake around a campfire drinking wine coolers under the evergreens and galaxies of stars.

The cherry blossom festival by the Kintai bridge with woodfired octopus smoke filling the frigid air.

Riding the trolley in the vibrant city of San Francisco - all the sourdough and sardines.

Of course there was the hayride under a harvest moon with hard cider and a young woman.

Fishing for rainbows in the White Mountains with friends and family.

The pungent smell of pot and the deafening music from Guns and Roses and Iron Maiden among fast friends.

Playing a trumped solo in front of a large crowd.

The birth of my son despite the anguish to come later.

Ah yes, later, like in a cold hospital getting picked apart by devilish souls and prison - dreams deferred - and prison, and no longer a happier consumer of life, no longer asymptomatic.

Wide Angle View

Of all things big I try to eschew
there is nothing more poignant than a wide angle view.

Now I see forests change with the season
As for youthful exuberance, a single frog, was a reason.

And now I see many when one was once enough
attempting to prioritize has become tough.

Time no longer marches - it's more like a gait
All bumpy and jerky with all of my weight.

What of all the shows and the media used to tell
Now a click of the mouse is something to sell.

So we work at globally connected stations
the wealth of our people the envy of nations.

Unfortunately it is said
that younger in our lives, than our parents, we're dead.

Somewhere along the line in life we lose our focus
Drowning our misery in Vente non-fat mochas.

So give me one thing at a time and tell me what's what
I'll give you a rhyme then keep my mouth shut.

If I had any advice for you
It's stay away from that wide angle view.

In Between

In between birth and death poetry finds us maturing with every line. Whether it be self-perceived or borrowed from the greats, poetry gives us the propensity to absorb life as it is or might be.

Regardless of our predisposition, when we first encounter it, the lines perhaps with the silence as well as sound or rather the stuff of life gives us all the more reason to appreciate it. As for me, I have found many favorite lines that are so eloquent and self-pertinent I really do, in the end, find myself between them. By way of example:

Marianne Moore writes in <u>Poetry</u>

"I too dislike it. Reading it, however, with a perfect contempt for it, one discovers in it, after all, a place for the genuine."

One would think after my heinous crime that there would be no poetry left. In a way there isn't. Somehow, though, I can still find joy in between the lines – a genuine fondness. For instance, Frost could not possibly have known that when he wrote the lines:

"When I see birches bend to left and right, across the lines of straighter darker trees..."

that I would remember the grandparents' birches with the snow covered bird feeder swarming with finches, chickadees, robins and all the other birds. Likewise when Langston Hughs writes:

"I heard the singing of the Mississippi
when Abe Lincoln went down to New
Orleans, and I've seen its muddy bottom
turn all golden in the sunset."

It's as if he held my hand walking down Beale Street, past the blues houses to overlook the river myself from another famous southern city but it strikes me well all the same.

Then Sherman Alexie writes:

"That salmon leaps into the night air above the water, throws a lightening bolt at the brush near my feet, and starts the fire."

One simply must see a salmon making a jumping journey upstream and all of the magical qualities I ascribed to fish as a boy, come alive.

Now that I age I remember a quote that successful people hold on to death like a rock; and Gregory Orr writes:

"Childhood dotted with bodies
Let them go, Let them
be ghosts.
No, I said,
make them stay, make them stone."

Almost literally, in the end as of now, I fall somewhere in between the lines; so it is that even a convict can appreciate the form and mature and learn one poem at a time, to choose between ghosts and stone.

Coda

One more phrase before the end
voices and opinions we'd strive to lend

There was quite a bit of gold to find
yet some was better suited to swine

Each of us had our own style
with a verve all would beguile

Some was written that was spiritual
and some described a dream miracle

Stories long and short we heard
amazing what can come from the simple word

The group deadline and participation
ensured productivity and elation

Anodyne island of sanity in it's own way
- but as Frost imparted to us -
"Nothing gold can stay."

Changels

We are the afterburden in a chrysalis
dangerously mortal and chasing peace of mind
They are the stewards of souls
and as we suffer some psychic potential
they can make dreams come true
When they move out west
all roads lead to Hollywood and Vine
debating which to eschew and which to keep
never taking criticism well
You get giggles on the sidewalk
and then you move on.

Mind the Wind

The black clad terrorists
march down an Iraqi street
like a high school marching band
only a little self conscious
and full of verve and weapons.
I glance again at the singular
black and white newspaper photo
that emotes concern for all.
Uniforms are the new black.
Black like oil, the currency of the soul,
Black as the smoke of a car bomb
taking life and limb.
Noxious; greasy, gore, seasoned hate
Black as the char in the rubble.
With or without a bomb,
it's little wonder that
suicide is the new black.
But, black, MLK and a promise of
a post-racist paradigm,
maybe? Not yet.
No way to join the fight
without a shadow all our own,
skin crawling reality
Gut wrenching hell-inspired
shadow spilling out.
A thousand year old feud.
Yet we, as the contemporary devil,
afraid of what it might mean to lose
must mind the wind
that scatters the ashes.

Autumn of Life

On the best overcast Autumn day
trees are turning - the world is churning.

From the hospital window the turkey vultures
circle above the iconic changing leaves.
When they circle over me I change as well.

Amidst the oaks and sycamore
the vultures forewarn of death thusly
not many days left I'm guessing.

The poison in my mind is no longer enough
completely boxed in again in a hospital.

A place for healing and stealing one and the same
though it lingers in my mind like cancer.

The brain chemistry is off they say
But it's a voice that ruins a truly good day
and so the phantom pains persist and my heart is the gist
some perverted being likes to torture and set up ridicule.

And laugh they do
as if my demise is just funny
only so long as they can do it again on the morrow
when we will meet in the hall anywhere
and I will be hurt for not following the invisible script.

Not follow it for awhile and you will lose
your health, family, friends
most anything you wanted to keep
and trust me you'll weep
when the cataclysmic realization hits
and tells you no more life for you
no script as true
mandatory suicide they say.

Twenty-fourth Street USA

It all begins and ends here
24th Street can take you away
past pools, schools, and dentists
to the hospital
Graffiti on cinderblock walls
smacks of class struggle
The taste of blowing sand
in this arid land is palpable
and four Circle K's from beginning
to end – conveniences
like layers of grime covering
my grave through the years
where I am ancient and mineral once again.

To Touch a Soul

Father

Did they hold a son at birth?

Hands that played military speed Yahtzee
Fireplace illuminated the tumble of dice
with full reason and family
of young and old hands together for a night
fading like dying red embers
Soon to be those no one remembers
What to do with invisible hands?

Did they toil in the fields?

cutting vines and pitching melons
moving down the rows as swift as able
stooped over the harvest, effort in repetition
invisible hands sending food to the table
tanned and callused by the elements and exertion
earning a pittance and unknown by convention
What to do with invisible hands?

Did they ever touch her cheek, the
woman you knew and loved
but just missed by an eternity?

Held a lover close on the log ride
Spray of water crashing at the end
Essence of Her in the artifical tide
hold hands in stride to do it again
losing grasp of her hand to another
left with invisible hands like a brother

What to do with invisible hands?

Did they play catch in the great halls?

Hands that may have saved your life
swimming, driving, working, writing
now locked away behind the back in strife
Imprisoned, these hands no longer inviting
finally, as invisible as is possible to be
Almost, as if this life were waiting for me
What to do with invisible hands?

Did they ever touch anything more tangible than a soul?

American Ascension

A campfire spark rising
miniature tempest darting up in a whorl
Aspiring to the eagle's eye
A glint known by the Firefly
offers up our fleeting spirituals to the sky
while cutting off quarter inches of our single pixel lives
to expose the schism in our minds
so that we might deal with it there
lest it infect our hearts
We let it go and go, up and up
until the work causing our distraction
is rendered, and keeps us wondering,
wandering out of sight.

The End

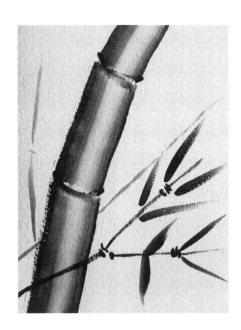

About the Author

The author is forty-eight and has a BSBA from the University of Arizona. The work was created over a period of three years. The artwork is by the author. Another literary work is in progress.

Edwards Brothers Malloy
Ann Arbor MI. USA
July 18, 2016